From New York City

To the World

-Let's remind ourselves-

Daniela Hoeche

Published by Lulu.com 2010
Copyright © Daniela Hoeche 2009

ISBN: 978-1-4457-5565-6

Cover picture: © PantherMedia/Lars P.

We are individuals, a creation of ourselves. Like a black & white picture, we would look dead without colors. We are homeless when we don't build the house of the fundament that was given to us. In a black & white picture, is everything shown that should be shown? In our lives, is everything given that should be given? We can build on this fundament. We can give the picture colors to let it live just as we can give ourselves colors to glare in our whole beauty. God started the creation of the world and gave us everything we need to go on with what he started. Just as trees have to grow by themselves, we have to grown by ourselves. Life is not about finding ourselves, it is about creating us. It is about making the best of everything that has been given to us.

Content

Acknowledgments

One of the greatest joys in creating this book has been meeting people from all over the world. They gave this project heart & soul. Their stories and experiences gave me the inspiration, new views, knowledge and so much positivity and encouragement to write this book. Thank you for sharing your lives with me.

I would like to thank my parents Maria and Helmut and my sister Angie, who have given me love and support throughout this project. You are my engine and inspiration and I love you more than words can describe. I also want to thank Darrell Warden Jr. and his family for their endless belief in me, and for the love and encouragement they have given me... I love you. I would also like to thank Wayne for his support and belief. Thank you to all my mentors I have met on this journey, you let me grow. I would also like to thank D. Miller, for giving me the reason to start writing this book.

I would like to thank all the people who will read this book, you give my words life and meaning the moment you read them. Without you, they could never live!

Introduction

Welcome to New York, the city where everything is possible. It's the city where you can feel the energy when you walk through the streets. Love and hate are so close together. No city in this world has so much energy. No city moves so fast. It is never standing still. New York is alive 24/7. I love New York City! A lot of people do the same thing… they all come to "The Big Apple" to realize their dreams. If you really want to realize your dreams in this city, you have to face it. You have to know who you are and what you want.

That is what this book is about. It's about learning to be you. I have seen a lot, and I have gone through a lot, but I am at a point where I can say that I am not afraid anymore to be myself. I am proud of the person that I am. It was a long journey to get to this point, but it was an interesting journey. If I could go back in time, I would do everything like I did before because it made me the person I am today. Ladies and Gentlemen, remind yourselves what life is about. Learn how to handle your emotions to help make your journey through life the best it can be. Follow your road without fear. Follow your curiosity; it will bring you to places you have never been before. You will always meet good, as well as bad people, but both have one thing in common; they will influence your life. Take everything that happens to you as an experience and grow with it. You need to make mistakes to learn what's good for you. When you were a child you heard the sentence from your parents, "Don't do that", but you did it and realized it was not good for you, and stopped doing it. Experiences, personal decisions, and the consequences which come with it, let us grow. Now that we are adults, we are afraid to make mistakes. We think it's something bad, something we have to be ashamed of. If we never make mistakes and we never fail, how will we grow? How will we live our lives like we want to? Firstly, it should not matter to you what others think about you. If you fail, it's something you have to deal with and nobody else. I have learned that it is important to do my thing without listening to others all the time. In the end, I am the person who has to live with it! I have learned that it doesn't matter what we look like, whether we are rich or poor, famous or not, we all have to deal with the same feelings. We all know love, anger, pain. This book is a book that everybody can identify with, and that makes it something normal and so special at the same time. You can laugh and cry because you can face yourself. You will see what life is about. This book will take you on a wonderful journey that will change your life. It will change your life because you will change. I am glad to share all of this with you. I am not a psychologist and I don't claim to be one. I just want to remind you of what you already know. Let the journey start!

I think it's time to remind ourselves what life is actually about, to give us back the positive feelings and take away the negative ones. This book contains advice to help you control yourself, to steer you in the right direction. When you have achieved that, you don't have to be afraid of situations in life deviating you from your way anymore. It doesn't matter what happens in your life, you will all be able to stand and face every feeling without losing yourself. This is a wonderful thought, isn't it? And the best thing is; it costs us nothing.

We live in a material world; everybody is looking for more - more money, more success. It is exactly this yearning that causes us to forget about things that actually matter in life. We are not satisfied with what we have. We are not taking enough care of it. No, we are focused on getting more! I also love all these material things, but I would never forget to be thankful for everything good I have in my life - healthiness, love, family and friends. These things are too important for me to forget about.

We need to develop strong personalities so we don't care what others think of us. Material things are our business cards to show people how successful we are. Strong people don't need to show it. It's enough that they know how successful they are themselves. Oh, by the way: What actually is the definition of success? It lies in the eye of the beholder. Nobody can say where success starts. But one thing is for sure, if you have a strong personality, you will be successful your whole life because you know what you want and don't care what others think about you. We really need to find out what we really want and who we really are, because when we are not able to face ourselves, how shall we face others?

The following chapters show the most important emotions, and in which situations you have to deal with them in your life. You can't run away, you have to control your emotions, otherwise they will control you. You will remind yourself and you will change into a new person, a stronger person, a person who is able to go this road through life powerfully and fearlessly!

From New York City to the world,
Let us remind ourselves!

Change

They always say time changes things, but you actually have to change them yourself.
Andy Warhol, The Philosophy of Andy Warhol
US artist (1928 - 1987)

Only I can change my life. No one can do it for me.
Carol Burnett, US actress & comedienne (1936 -)

If the facts don't fit the theory, change the facts.
Albert Einstein, (attributed), US (German-born) physicist
(1879 - 1955)

Human beings, by changing the inner attitudes of their minds, can change the outer aspects of their lives.
William James, US Pragmatist philosopher & psychologist
(1842 - 1910)

You can't stand it? Then change it!

Every one of us wants to live in a better world, but only a few of us actually do anything to better it. I can't change people, but I can try to show them that every one of us is able to make a change, a change for others, and for oneself. When you believe in yourself, you will be able to find solutions for the problems you have. Every one of us is able to make a change, and in my opinion, it's everybody's job to do it because we all live here. Everybody has to do their part, their job, to make this world the best it can be. I am not famous, I am not rich, but I am able to talk to people and explain to them about the problems we have, to open their eyes hoping they will see and start changing something. We all can't stand the fact that people suffer because of hunger. We all can't stand the fact that people are still discriminated against. We all can't stand the politics of our country, but we don't do anything to change these things. Can anyone explain to me, how can things improve if no one feels a responsibility to do something? If everyone would give one dollar a month to people who have nothing to eat, believe me, these people wouldn't have to think about hunger anymore. If everyone would accept that we are all different, our religions, our skin color and our thoughts, we wouldn't have discrimination anymore. If everyone would go to the polls, we wouldn't have the wrong people in politics anymore. Easy, isn't it? Just with these few things you can change a lot. We are responsible for our lives and we are responsible for our world, but we must act. We have to do something to affect change. It's not easy to face all these problems we have, but it's still easier than to live with them. Every time there is a catastrophe, people stand together and help. We shouldn't always wait for catastrophes; we should try to avoid what we can avoid. We can't always wake up after things have already happened. We have to wake up before! To avoid situations, to change situations, to stand up for what we believe in, we need strong personalities and we need to be able to handle our emotions. This is something you can learn. You can see your life positively or negatively, it's up to you. You have the choice. The glass can be half full or half empty. Just with this one thought you can decide, whether you still have something (positive) or whether you are losing something (negative). One thing is for sure, the more you see your life positively, the more you are going to be successful and the more you are going to be satisfied. It's so simple! Change the things in your life that you don't like. Do you really think a problem disappears by itself and that your life brings itself into the right direction? I promise you that will never happen! You have to work on yourself constantly to achieve a happy and satisfied life. You should learn that change can be something good, something you don't have to be afraid of. Only those who have fear can be courageous. Life is a challenge, and it's precisely this challenge that you have to meet, otherwise you will exist, but never live. Patience is important for things we can't influence, but all that we can influence, we should influence. Don't wait any longer to remind yourself, and learn to steer your life in the right direction!

The Past

Those who cannot remember the past are condemned to repeat it.

George Santayana, The Life of Reason, Volume 1, 1905, US (Spanish-born) philosopher (1863 - 1952)

To regret the past is to forfeit the future.

Chinese Proverb

Even God cannot change the past.

Agathon, (448 BC - 400 BC)

Shut out all of your past except that which will help you weather your tomorrows.

Sir William Osler, British (Canadian-born) physician (1849 - 1919)

Be thankful for yesterday, appreciate today and you will see the beauty of tomorrow!

Actually, I would say, "live in the present don't look back or forward". Sometimes, it's important to look back to be able to understand why you are the person you are. Our childhood is the period of our lives in which we grow faster than any other period. It's the time in which we build our personalities, in which we learn the most about ourselves. It's the period in which we are growing so fast that we can't save everything in our heads. It's like text messages in our cell phones; we have to delete some of them from time to time, to make room to save new incoming messages. It's the same thing that we're doing with our memories. We have deleted a lot of memories in our heads to save the incoming ones. But by asking the people we grew up with, we can remind ourselves about things we have forgotten about. We should make this journey back to find out what happened in our past, why we are the person we are today, and which problems we still carry with us. When we understand and remember our past, we can clean up our present, and look forward to our future. Otherwise, you can be sure that your past will follow you into your future.

When you make this journey back, you should never forget this; never regret what you did in the past, you can't change it, you can just take it as another lesson learned and grow with it. Earlier in my life I was ashamed of things I did, and I often thought about why I had done them. Today, I laugh about it and say to myself: "that was stupid but anyway, it will not happen again". When someone confronts me with it I will say: "Yes, I did those things, I made those mistakes, what about it"? I am a human being not a machine. Believe me, to accept the fact that we make mistakes, that we are not perfect, is going to make us very strong people because we have nothing to hide. We are courageous enough to be ourselves. We are honest to ourselves, and that's the basis of being honest to others. So don't be afraid, make this journey back into your past and learn who you are. It's going to be exiting. After this journey, your life will change because your views about yourself will change. Changes are good, they bring us forward in life and we want to go forward, don't we?

Opinion

Our opinions do not really blossom into fruition until we have expressed them to someone else.

Mark Twain, quoted in Mark Twain and I, Opie Read, 1940 US humorist, novelist, short story author, & wit (1835 - 1910)

An opinion can't be a wrong answer!

By growing older and becoming adults, we lose nearly all the important traits we possess as children. When we ask a child for their opinion, we will get an honest answer. The child doesn't think about how we feel, or what our opinion could be. No, the child just gives us an answer to our question. Simple, isn't it? If we ask an adult, the adult will think about it first before giving an answer. The fear of what could happen by giving the wrong answer is too great. But what is a "wrong" answer? If somebody asks us about our opinion, how could it be wrong to say what we think? We have a problem being ourselves. We enter school and lecturers teach us to be serious, to get integrated within the environment. Teachers and responsible people in our lives tell us when we fail, when we are not good enough. They also teach us that if no one gives us a chance, we will never achieve what we want to achieve. Adults should support children's uniqueness and individual personalities, instead of having them conform simply to function within society. We shouldn't encourage our children to lose all the good qualities, and having one's own opinion is a good quality.

If someone asks you for your opinion, just give an answer without fear and doubt about what others might think. It can't be wrong to tell a person what you think about something or someone. Have you ever thought about the fact that this person needs another view to go ahead with a decision on something, or someone, and that this person chose you to aid them in their decision? You are important enough to this person that they want to hear your opinion rather than that of someone else? Perceive it as positive if someone wants to know your opinion because you are worthy enough, and can be taken seriously. To have your own opinion is important because it shows that you stand for something, and behind something. This attribute is something for which people give you respect for. It's called personality! Have enough faith in yourself and the things you are committed to, then you will never have a problem expressing yourself and saying what you think. You are going to be an important adviser for people in your environment, in your private, as well as in your business life.

Remember: When you want to be successful, it's a precondition to be able to advance an opinion!

Answers to questions

A thinker sees his own actions as experiments and questions--as attempts to find out something. Success and failure are for him answers above all.

Friedrich Nietzsche, The Gay Science, section 41, German philosopher (1844 - 1900)

It is better to know some of the questions than all of the answers.

James Thurber, US author, cartoonist, humorist, & satirist (1894 - 1961)

The value of the question

We ask questions but we don't always get answers. Is it so important to always get an answer? I don't think so. I think it's much more important to know what we want in life; to know what we feel apart from the answers to our questions. We should stop questioning everything! Sometimes it's just what it is… another question without an answer!

Asking questions is our way of receiving knowledge, which is important to us. Whoever has knowledge can understand. Questions are important, they help us learn and grow, but sometimes you have to differentiate between situations in life where the answer will not change the attitude towards a person or situation. It has no learning-effect. Try not to question everything in life. When talking about feelings, you will feel and see it. You don't always need words to prove what you already know inside of yourself. Trust your gut!!! Accept what you can't change and change what you can influence. Respect when you don't get an answer to your question. Achieve a learning-effect by questioning and don't search for approval of things you already know, or a question which you will never get an answer to. If I want to know what someone thinks about this book, and I know that they have read it, but I am too embarrassed or afraid to know their true opinion of it, I might ask them if they have read it hoping they will give me the opinion that I am looking for. However, more often than not, I probably will only get the answer to my question and nothing more. I will still not know what they think about my book. Therefore, I questioned something without any results. I got an answer to something I already knew. This is what I call wasted time. You can't expect that someone will read your mind to find out what your intention was with your question. The person will just answer according to your question. If the question is explicit, the answer will be more accurate. When I ask the mentioned person what they think about the book I have written and the person lets me know their opinion, I have accomplished my intention and I have achieved a learning-effect.

Remember: Don't question everything, and if you question, do it as accurately as you are able to, in order to accomplish your intentions and give therewith a meaning to your questions.

Knowledge

Knowledge is discovered, when ignorance is lost.

Jason F. Klein, "As life is written", Sonoma State University (1992)

Through wisdom is a house builded; and by understanding it is established: And by knowledge shall the chambers be filled with all precious and pleasant riches.

The Bible (KJV), Proverbs 24:4

Only those, who have knowledge, are able to understand!

Knowledge is the basis for everything. It is the fundament on which we build our houses. Without it, a house could never stand. Knowledge of yourself and your environment is important because only those who have knowledge are able to understand, and we all want to understand, don't we? It removes fears and prejudices, and helps us to see the backgrounds of various behaviors and situations. It gives us self-confidence and power. It's the answer to our questions. It's timeless and endless. We can keep it, or share it. It doesn't matter which plan you have made for your life, it is unpredictable and you have to expect the unexpected. Therefore, it is more important to handle your emotions, and with them, the different situations in life. Unexpected situations will be easier to handle with certain knowledge. It enables us to find solutions for the challenges life brings us. It gives us the feeling of certainty. The more knowledge you have, the more possibilities you have. Fear and prejudice occur because of nescience. For example, if you are afraid of spiders, you will avoid every situation in which you might come in contact with a spider. But when you start learning about spiders, they would probably still be disgusting to you, but you would recognize that there is actually no reason to be afraid of spiders. Another example of missing knowledge is prejudice. People prejudge others because they don't know any better. They have never tried to understand the backgrounds of behaviors, situations or cultures. Nobody has taught them to question these things. If they had knowledge they would understand and thus, would never prejudge anything, or anyone. You don't have to accept everything in life, but knowledge will teach you to respect it. Life is so exciting, there is so much to discover. The way of knowledge is a never-ending journey, and with every trip we take we grow a little bit more. Take this journey and learn! Do it for you, and change to a fearless and positively thinking person.

Remember: Who knows his nescience is exalted, but who perceives it for knowledge is in agony.

Passion

Only passions, great passions, can elevate the soul to great things.

Denis Diderot, French author, encyclopedist, &
philosopher (1713 - 1784)

Nothing great in the world has been accomplished without passion.

Georg Wilhelm, O Magazine, September 2003

The heart of emotions is the way to success!

Passion is the heart of emotions. According to author and journalist Thomas Friedman, passion and curiosity are key components for education in a world where information is readily available to everyone and where global markets reward those who have learned how to learn and are self-motivated to learn.

Friedman's proposed formula is: Curiosity Quotient plus Passion Quotient is greater than Intelligent Quotient.

Friedman states, "Give me the kid with a passion to learn and a curiosity to discover and I will take him or her over the less passionate kid with a huge IQ every day of the week." IQ "still matters, but CQ and PQ ... matter even more." ...

References: Curious George and A Formula for Lifelong Learning: CQ + PQ > IQ, Brigham Young University.

Friedman further states that, "it is more important to be passionate and curious than to be merely smart."

Yet another author, Virender Kapoor says, "It is not Intelligence Quotient (IQ) but your Passion Quotient (PQ) that will take you to the pinnacle of success."

References: Deccan Herald article on Passion Quotient: The way to reach greater heights June 13, 2007

Passion is a feeling of unusual excitement or enthusiasm about a subject, idea, person, or object. It is the fire that burns within us. It's the strongest feeling that exists. It comprehends every emotion. Passion is the heart of emotions. We develop it subconsciously... it is present. Passion is power and it gives us power. I love it and I live it! When you have it, your charisma is going to fascinate your environment. People will be focussed on you. It makes you attractive to others. Passion shows confidence. Passion is our drive. Your environment is attracted to you without knowing what it is that attracts it. They will not question it, because they feel good when you are around. They are going to be addicted to the feeling you give them. You are able to receive the attention of others without effort. You will get chances others won't get. This aura lets you shine even in the dark. Passion is to be alive ... it is life. By showing your passion, you show yourself. By living your passion, you live your life. It's going to make you successful, knowledgeable and satisfied. You will see things others will never see. You will feel things others will never feel. Every time you are sad and cry, every time you love and get drunk with this feeling, every time you can't give up trying to achieve a goal, it's passion that is talking to you. When you are passionate, I can promise you that your life will be everything but boring; not for you and not for your environment. You will live every moment intensively. You will scream when you're angry, cry when you're sad and laugh when you're happy.

Remember: Passion lets you shine. It comes from the bottom of your heart, a place nobody can see, but you make it visible and that makes you special!!!

Success

Success usually comes to those who are too busy to be looking for it.

Henry David Thoreau, US Transcendentalist author
(1817 - 1862)

You always pass failure on the way to success.

Mickey Rooney, US actor (1920 -)

Success is the ability to go from one failure to another with no loss of enthusiasm.

Sir Winston Churchill, British politician (1874 - 1965)

Constant work is constant success!

How do we actually define success? A woman who stays at home and has an organized household can define this as success. A businessman who has been promoted to a higher level can also tout success. These are examples of two different people, two different definitions. Success is the achievement of the goals we have defined for ourselves. This makes success something personal. It can't be right or wrong, nor is there an age limit, heritage, skin colour, financial status or religion. Simply, the constant work for our goals brings us success. I am confident that you have been successful many times in your life without recognizing it because these achievements were not considerable enough that you gave them meaning. We should celebrate each success, even the little ones, as if we have won Academy Awards. With celebrating, we will remind ourselves of what we have already achieved in our lives and motivate ourselves. This will give us the confidence and power to stay strong in every weak moment in our lives. The more you are willing to do something for your goal, the more successful you will be in life. This is not about believing in it, it is about working for it.

Success, the realization of your dreams, is not something that comes immediately. It is a long road, full of mistakes, decisions and disappointments. Only those who don't lose their goal on the way, those who believe in it, and work for it, are going to achieve it. When you run a marathon, the way you run from the start to the end is the strategy that helps you achieve your goal. It doesn't matter where you were standing at the beginning, or when you reach the end, what counts is the long way of efforts you left behind to get there. Every step on your way is important, no matter how long it takes. Patience is what keeps your head free from stress and pressure. From the moment in which you understand it and live it, you will see that every step brings you closer to your goal. A free mind allows you to make the right decisions. Whatever interrupts you on your way, grow with it and see it as your development to get smarter, stronger and becoming unstoppable. The times you grow the most are the worst and most difficult times in your life. You achieve the best learning effect during these times because they influence you the most. Use this power to turn the negative aspects into positive ones to make the impossible possible.

Make a list and write down your goals with all the necessary steps. Place this list where you can see it every day. It will support you and remind you. It is an open list, which is waiting to be closed. Work hard and constantly on it. Learn to take risks. Learn to sacrifice. Without any input, you will not achieve anything.

Never forget that success is personal, it is about YOUR goal, so let others think whatever they want to think, it's your life and you define your goals...you and nobody else. So, go and be successful in everything you do!

Envy

Envy can be a positive motivator. Let it inspire you to work harder for what you want.

Robert Bringle, quoted in Redbook

Love looks through a telescope; envy, through a microscope.
Josh Billings, US Humorist (1818 - 1885)

Maybe it's easier to like someone else's life, and live vicariously through it, then take some responsibility to change our lives into lives we might like.

Tish Grier, love and hope and sex and dreams, 04-12-2006

Love yourself the way you are and envy will stay far away!

Envy is an emotion that is not necessary, an emotion that blocks us in our view of life. It makes us blind to our own lives because we are too focused on other people's lives. We can't stand that others have something we don't have. We can't stand it because we are not satisfied with our lives. Instead of changing something to make it better, or accepting that we are who we are, we become envious of things and abilities others own. But shouldn't we learn to accept the fact that we can't have everything? We can admire people for things they have achieved in life, but envy is a very negative feeling which causes us to react negatively, and we want to stay positive, don't we? We should learn to admire instead of being envious. We should also give ourselves a chance. When we learn to love ourselves for who we are, we would not feel envy anymore, because we would be thankful for everything we have in our lives. We came to this world the way God intended us, and to play God and try to change everything about ourselves, concerning our personalities, won't make us happy. Every person has a talent. There are people who can sing, others are good in writing. Find your own talent and focus on it. Find your way in life and don't waste your time with being envious. Accept yourself for who you are and be proud of it.

We are envious of things and talents others have, but have you ever thought about what they don't have? We are envious of famous people. We see the attention they receive, see the money they earn, but we don't see the price they have to pay for their fame. If we compared their lives to ours, we would discover that the price they have to pay for it is high. We pick out all the good things about their lives because envy blocks our minds. We don't see the negative aspects. Why can't we do it for ourselves? Why can't we put the negative things in our lives away to see the positive ones? We would see all the good things we have in our lives. We would see and find our talents. We wouldn't be envious anymore, and would be grateful for who we are and what we have. Be happy for others and everything good they have achieved. This gives us a better feeling. Life is a benchmark. Learn from others and improve. Lose the negative feeling "envy" and use the chance to learn and grow.

It's your life. Don't waste your time with negative emotions, they are not necessary. Live your life as best as you can and love yourself, as well as others. Get out of this chain of emotions. They are not good for you. These negative emotions only divert you from your way and let you forget about who you really are.

Anger

Anger is the feeling that makes your mouth work faster than your mind.

Evan Esar, *American Humorist (1899 - 1995)*

When anger rises, think of the consequences.

Confucius, Chinese philosopher & reformer (551 BC - 479 BC)

Talk about anger to let it go

Anger turns into hate when you don't control it. It is a human reaction towards everything, and everyone that has hurt and disappointed us. We are humans, and of course we are vulnerable, but we should just be vulnerable up to a certain point. We have to learn to avoid people who give us negative feelings. Someone can only make us angry when we allow them to make us angry. We have to find out for ourselves why people make it possible for us to become angry. Children especially have a big problem with anger. They need adults as people they can talk to. They need our experience and our advice. But most of us don't have enough time for our children anymore. In the past, mothers stayed at home to take care of the family. Today, the financial situation often doesn't allow it to be this way, so mothers have to work. Therefore, children often raise themselves nowadays. Children need a person to trust, a person who shows them the way through life, a person who gives them boundaries. When this person is absent, what ends up happening is that children try to find ways by themselves to handle their anger...the wrong ways. They start getting aggressive, start to hate, and start to get violent. They are looking for ways to get their negative feelings out of them. I know it is not easy, but when you have children, you have a responsibility and you should take it seriously. We have to make sure that we have enough time for their problems. We should be there for them with a shoulder to cry on. We should never judge them, but rather teach them. I went to anger groups in churches to learn more about anger. I was shocked when I learned how many people were killed on our streets because of anger, hate and violence. I was even more shocked when I heard how many people would do the same to the people responsible for these senseless acts. We have to fight against anger more than ever before to avoid it, so it does not transform into hate, and develop into violence. It is a big and serious problem, but it's in our hands to stop it, and to also help others handle it. When you go to an anger group in church and listen to the people and to their stories, you will understand what I mean. Once you realize the severity of what I am talking about, I bet you will start to change something. In my mind, I can still picture these people. They are all so different, but all have the same problem. I will keep these pictures there, because they motivate me to go on and make a change. I will not sit here and watch it worsen! I will help to stop it at the basis, because the next steps we are talking about are even more dangerous and even more serious. With our behavior, we have to show ourselves, our families, friends and especially our children, how anger should be handled. With only this little step, you will change a lot. God gave us a mouth to talk, when we are angry we should use this mouth to talk about it. When we talk about our anger, we have the chance to avoid aggression, because we let it out. If we do not, we will start to hate. Find a way to handle your anger. Do something! Don't keep it inside hoping that it disappears after a while. It will always be in your mind if you don't try to get rid of it.

Hate

If you hate a person, you hate something in him that is part of yourself. What isn't part of ourselves doesn't disturb us.

Hermann Hesse, Swiss (German-born) author (1877 - 1962)

We hate some persons because we do not know them; and we will not know them because we hate them.

Charles Caleb Colton, (1780 - 1832)

Always remember others may hate you but those who hate you don't win unless you hate them. And then you destroy yourself.

Richard M. Nixon, in his White House farewell
37th president of US (1913 - 1994)

Don't give hate a chance

We shouldn't get into a circle of negative feelings to the point at which the bomb explodes. We moved from envy, over anger, to hate. We develop negativity, because we carry open issues with us. When someone makes us sad and we avoid crying, even though we feel like it, we start to act, and with it, we start to hate. We blame the person that made us sad for these negative feelings. Instead of venting, we begin to act out. We bring ourselves to this point, not anyone else. How can we give someone else the fault? Tears, which come out and disappear, are better than hate, which stays. We should not hate someone for something that is our own fault because we are not able to let it out, to live our feelings. It's easy to give someone else the blame instead of changing something about us. We have to change ourselves and should not expect that others change for us. We have to learn to let our emotions go and avoid thinking negatively as much as we can. We already talked about being envious. Envy is a feeling we can replace with admiration. We go from a negative view to a positive view, changing the whole situation by changing our perspective. Hate is something we don't need to replace, because we should not let it come to the point at which we develop it. We have so many problems in this world, we certainly don't need more. Hate is a problem, so we should try to avoid it. We have to learn not to view it as something worse to let our feelings out, and not view it as something weak to show our feelings to others. Most of us learned it from home when our parents said: Be strong, don't cry, or: Don't be so angry, that's impolite. We learned that it's weak to cry and impolite to be angry. We should immediately forget what we have learned, because it's not true! A person who cries when they're sad is strong. We should see these people as strong people, because they live their emotions without fearing what others think about them. Perfect! This is exactly the right way. We shouldn't care about whether others think we're weak or impolite, it's our body and we have to live with it. If there is something bothering us and we want to let it out, then we should let it out and let it go. If we didn't care about people, we wouldn't hate people. In accordance, not caring about people is not paying attention, and by hating someone we pay attention, negative attention, but attention. Love and hate are close together, even if it sounds weird. We should avoid letting a wonderful feeling like love turn into a negative feeling like hate. It's in our hands! Keep the love and throw the hate away, or else you will use a very dangerous way to let it out, and this way is called violence!

Violence

Returning violence for violence multiplies violence, adding deeper darkness to a night already devoid of stars... Hate cannot drive out hate: only love can do that.
Martin Luther King Jr., US black civil rights leader &
clergyman (1929 - 1968)

I object to violence because when it appears to do good, the good is only temporary; the evil it does is permanent.
Mahatma Gandhi, Indian political and spiritual leader
(1869 - 1948)

No society that feeds its children on tales of successful violence can expect them not to believe that violence in the end is rewarded.

Margaret Mead, Anthropologist (1901-1978)
US anthropologist & popularizer of anthropology (1901 -
1978)

When we sum envy, anger and hate up, we get violence as a result.

When we come to the point at which we start to get violent, we have a serious problem and need help. As discussed, it's a long way to violence and it's difficult to get away from it. Violence grows over years. We have to find out why we are unsatisfied with ourselves and our lives, why we have so much hate in ourselves. It will not be easy, but it's possible. We have to learn to face ourselves. We have to learn to handle our anger. We have to find ways to let our anger out. Ways like talking, instead of swallowing things that bother us, or going to the gym instead of punching someone. Violence is just a way people use to let their negative emotions go, to let them out. Hurting others is the wrong way, and the biggest problem with it is that most of the time we hurt people we love, people who are close and important to us. We have our emotions in our hands, we can steer them…us and nobody else. If you have a problem with violence, you need someone to show you how to handle it. It is not weak to ask for help, it would be weak to not do it. You risk losing a lot of important people in your life if you do not learn to cope without becoming violent. They will leave because they can't stand to suffer because of you anymore. This should be the best motivation for you. Change yourself, stop hurting people you love. Would you rather end up all alone one day? Start with a positive view to find solutions for problems you have. Looking for help is a solution, because violence is a problem. When you learn to handle your negative emotions, the positive feeling you achieve in the end will give you a better life, a new life, and it will motivate others to do the same. We have to stop violence! Every one of us must help to stop it. Only when we fight against it as a unit, can we change something. We have to change ourselves to avoid getting violent and we have to help people, who can't find ways by themselves. There are so many organizations that fight against it day after day. Courageous people who have made it their jobs, and without them, we would have even more violence. When you want to have a better life, you can get it. You just have to accept the help from others who offer it to you. It will be a long way, but it will be exciting because you will start to see the positive things in life a little bit more day by day. You will learn to show your love again to the people who are so important to you. You will rediscover your dreams that you have forgotten about because of this hate you were busy with all the time. You will start to change your life and learn to realize your dreams. You will see that there will be no time for envy, anger, hate and violence anymore. You will be too busy with the organization of your future, of your dreams. Stop the violence and start living.

Dreams

So many of our dreams at first seem impossible, then they seem improbable, and then, when we summon the will, they soon become inevitable.

Christopher Reeve, From speech at Democratic National Convention, August 1996

Our life is composed greatly from dreams, from the unconscious, and they must be brought into connection with action. They must be woven together.

Anais Nin, US (French-born) author & diarist (1903 - 1977)

The future belongs to those who believe in the beauty of their dreams.

Eleanor Roosevelt, US diplomat & reformer (1884 - 1962)

Our truest life is when we are in our dreams awake.

Henry David Thoreau, US Transcendentalist author (1817 - 1862)

Dreams are there to realize them

One of my dreams was to write a book. I wanted to help. I wanted to show people what they are able to do, so I started writing to make my dream come true. It was a long way of insecurities, fears, struggles but I did it. What will happen with it in the end, who knows! It's not important how it ends, it's just important that I did it. Yes, I am proud of myself! It's a great feeling and this is everything that counts!

Sometimes our fears and insecurities stop us on our way to the realization of our dreams. However, we shouldn't think about it all the time. We should follow our feelings and start to realize our dreams. You have nothing to lose, but everything to win. Realize that your dream is always a gain and never a loss. I am sitting here on the floor of my apartment, typing line by line into my computer, and with every line I type, I am coming closer to making my dream come true. Don't waste too much time thinking about it; use the time to live it. There is no age limit, heritage or skin color, it's simply your dream, waiting to be realized. Believe in yourself then you will be able to achieve everything you have ever dreamt of. Your ambition comes directly from your heart and it doesn't matter what life brings, it will not stop you from realizing your dreams. Expect the unexpected because life is unpredictable. However your plan looks, life will interrupt it, but this shouldn't make you weaker, it should make you even stronger. With every challenge you are up to, you will grow. With every mistake you make, you will learn. With every loss, you will appreciate that you have even more. Use the love, the passion and the experiences life brings you to be unstoppable on your way to your dream. In the end, you live it instead of dreaming it. Work hard and you will achieve everything you dream for. A dream is not just about belief; it is about working for it. Dreams are important, but we should not dream our whole lives. We should open our eyes to let them come true, because dreams were made to come true. It shouldn't be something impossible, it should be something we carry with us in our hearts, a thought and a feeling that should give us the motivation we need to make it possible.

Thoughts become wishes, wishes become dreams and dreams become truth!

Trust

The only way to make a man trustworthy is to trust him.

Henry Stimson, US politician (1867 - 1950)

Trust men and they will be true to you; treat them greatly, and they will show themselves great.

Essays, Ralph Waldo Emerson, First Series: Prudence, 1841US essayist & poet (1803 - 1882)

When you really trust someone, you have to be okay with not understanding some things.

Real Live Preacher, Real Live Preacher weblog, 07-08-04 Anonymous author of RealLivePreacher.com

If you're not able to trust yourself, you can't trust others.

Love, friendships, and relationships: do you think all this would work constantly without trust? Without trust, we would never have a working and successful relationship privately, as well as occupationally. It is the basis we have to provide for every relationship in life, even the one to ourselves. A lack of self-confidence is a want of confidence in our abilities and skills. This lack prevents us from accomplishing our goals and trusting ourselves. When we are not even able to trust the person we can control the most, namely us, we are definitely not able to trust any other person in our lives. This makes our lives, and that of the people in our environment more complicated. Giving trust always has something to do with giving control away, which is always a risk, because we will never have a guarantee that the person we give it to is really worth it. Success is always connected with risks. There will never be a safe way you can go, just a way you have to go to achieve your goal. This way is unpredictable, but also necessary when you want to realize your dreams, achieve your goals, or just live a satisfied and successful life.

People are naturally skeptical, and sometimes it is good to look at a person or situation twice, because it has a protective effect. Trust is something that we all have to work to obtain. It's nothing you will receive at the beginning and nothing you should give away at the beginning. It always takes some time before you give it, or receive it. Time is important to learn more about the person. Trust is like a trophy someone special receives from us when that person has proven that he or she deserves it. It should show them how special they are to us. You don't have to, nor should you, give it away to everybody. It is reserved only for people who show you that they're worthy of receiving trust from you. A relationship will never be a good relationship if we don't have trust. A friendship will never be a good friendship if we can't have trust. We have to count on people who are important to us and who should count on us. Sometimes, even people who are not important to us, but important for us are deserving of our trust. Therefore, we need trust. We will always make wrong decisions, give trust to the wrong people, but the more wrong decisions we make, the more we are going to improve to make the right ones. Have faith in trust!

Haters

It is better to be hated for what you are than to be loved for what you are not.

Andre Gide, French critic, essayist, & novelist (1869 - 1951)

Haters confirm our success

If you have haters, you are already successful, or at least you have achieved something they want, but don't have. Haters are people who intend to stop us on our way, because they can't stand that we have accomplished something they haven't. They are envious that we are courageous, that we are strong and that we go our way fearlessly. Concerning the envy, they will do everything to make your life more complicated, but as always, it's up to you to let them. Open your eyes and listen to your gut. There will always be people who make our lives more difficult. We have to see it as a challenge that we have to deal with. When we have haters, and feel that envy is in the air, we can already be proud of ourselves. It's the reward for our efforts and our hard work when people show us attention, negative attention but attention. This always means that they see us and take us seriously otherwise, they wouldn't care about us.

Actually, we should have pity on these people. They are not satisfied with their own lives, but instead of changing their lives, they waste time with being focused on ours. Like the author Herbert Kaufman said: "Mind your own business and in time you'll have a business of your own to mind." It's good to admire people for what they have achieved in life instead of hating them. The result would be that one day someone admires them for their success. To all the haters out there, it's a pleasure that you hate us, because it shows us how successful we are. Thank you for it! We pray for you. We pray that you overcome your frustrations and that you will live a happy life of your own one day, a life without hate.

My motto: "Thanks to the haters for hating us and showing us day by day how successful we are! Pity you get for free, for envy you must work!

Fake people

Be courteous to all, but intimate with few,
and let those few be well tried before you
give them your confidence. True friendship
is a plant of slow grow, and must undergo
and withstand the shocks of adversity
before it is entitled to the appellation.
George Washington, First president of US (1732 - 1799)

Attention! Actors in our lives.

There's another type of people that come along with success…fake people. They will pop up together with success and stay as long as we are successful. In my opinion, nobody needs fake people! We need someone real around us, especially when we are successful. Believe me, we have so many fake people in business, we don't need them in our private lives as well. They want to shine in the light we have worked so hard for. Nobody needs people in life that suck up to us 24/7. We should be confident enough to give ourselves a good feeling. We need people we can count on and who are there for us in times when we need them. We need people who keep us down to earth. So, it's up to you, but please be careful with these people. They are actors in their own lives and that makes them very good in the part they act. They will try to make your advantage to theirs. They have made it their profession to get everything but do nothing.

Are these people truly happy? I don't know but one thing I know for sure, you can enjoy your success best, when you know that you have done something for it.

Friendship

*Friendship makes prosperity more shining
and lessens adversity by dividing and
sharing it.*

Cicero, On Friendship, 44 B.C.,Roman author, orator, &
politician (106 BC - 43 BC)

*No distance of place or lapse of time can
lessen the friendship of those who are
thoroughly persuaded of each other's worth.*

Robert Southey, English poet (1774 - 1843)

*In the sweetness of friendship; let there be
laughter and the sharing of pleasures. For in
the dew of little things the heart finds its
morning and is refreshed.*

Kahlil Gibran, Lebanese artist & poet in US (1883 - 1931)

Whoever has real friends will always stand up when he falls

Friendships are so important in life. They are relationships, which develop over a period of time. They grow with every year, with every experience one goes through. We have to take care of it so that we don't lose it one day. We should love our friends for being in our lives and being there for us when we need them. When we are feeling sad, they will show us the sunny side of life. When we are feeling weak, they will give us strength. When we can't trust anybody, we can trust them. They see and love us the way we really are. We can always count on real friends. We can laugh and cry with them. We can share every emotion with them. They are real to us, and keep us real. You can have numerous hard times in life, but when you have real friends, it doesn't matter. You will get through these times and always stand up with new power. We can't choose our families, and not everybody is lucky enough to have a family that is there for them. However, we can choose our friends and when we take care of them; they will be there our whole lives. Whoever doesn't have real friends in life is a poor person. It doesn't matter how rich you are, real friendship is something money can't buy. It's a wonderful feeling to know you have real friends because you know that no matter what happens in your life, these people will be there standing by your side, laughing and suffering with you. You don't have to play a role, you can just be yourself. This is something special and worthy, and you should treat it as such. You should think about friendships as a blessing, and the most important thing to remember…never forget about your friends. I don't know what I would do without my friends. I am confident that life would go on, but it would be a lonely and sad life. To share our emotions with people we love and trust is wonderful and it is important. It lets us talk things out and find things out. Together we are much stronger than alone, and even the pain we sometimes feel is just half as painful, when we have a real friend on our side.

I want to thank my friends for being there for me, for letting me share my life with them. You make me laugh and cry, angry and happy. You know me without words and love me for the person I am. I love you guys from the bottom of my heart!!!

Self-Confidence

Believe in yourself! Have faith in your abilities! Without a humble but reasonable confidence in your own powers you cannot be successful or happy
Norman Vincent Peale, US clergyman (1898 - 1993)

I was always looking outside myself for strength and confidence but it comes from within. It is there all the time.
Anna Freud, Austrian psychoanalyst & psychologist (1895 - 1982)

It is better to regret what you have done than doing nothing. It is better to take a consequence of a decision you have made than never having made one. It is better to live your dreams, than to dream it. It is better to have an opinion others don't like than to have none.

Self-confidence is the trust in you

Life is not about finding yourself, it's about creating you. You can run with the flow and be an actor in your own life, or you can create yourself and be an artist. How you present yourself is how others will see you.

We simply function within society and our thoughts are the thoughts of others. We open a magazine, which tells us what we should wear, talk about or eat. Society has written rules and we comply because we know that if we just do what they expect, we are going to be accepted. We are losing our individualities and also our personalities. How will you be respected when you don't even respect yourself enough to be yourself? How can others have trust in your skills when you don't have trust in your own abilities? Don't hide yourself behind rules others have written, write your own rules and show the world who you are. It doesn't matter how you look, where you come from, if you are rich or poor, famous or not, we all have to deal with the same emotions. We all know love, anger and pain. The knowledge about your emotions, the ability to steer your emotions, to live your emotions will bring you to the top. You can't fail, you can only make mistakes, which allows you to learn and grow. You can be a leader, or a follower. You hold the keys to success, happiness and satisfaction in your hands and it is up to you to open the door. Life is not unfair, it's just unpredictable, but when you know who you are and what you want you can overcome EVERY situation life brings without losing yourself. Don't search for something that is already there, just start to live and show it. Remind yourself about what life is all about and make your journey the best. Follow YOUR road without fears, just with a curiosity that will bring you to places you have never been before. Everything is going to be good the moment in which you understand what it means to just be yourself.

Don't try to be perfect, be yourself and you will be perfect!

Life can be very difficult with all the unexpected emotions it brings with it. You have to handle a lot of difficult situations and you have to make a lot of difficult decisions in your life. Therefore, it's important to believe in yourself and to stand behind decisions you make, and with all the consequences that come with it. The more self-confident we are, the more we will go our own way and the better suited we will be to achieve our goals. We will not lie, because we are not afraid to have our own opinions. We will not play, because we are not afraid to do what we want to do. We will be able to take responsibility, because we are able to stand behind every decision we make. To trust ourselves is more difficult than to trust others, but why? It's difficult, because we have fears of failing. To be confident means to go your own way without thinking about what other people might say, or think about you. You can't fail when you don't give yourself the feeling to fail, you can just make mistakes, and mistakes allow us to grow. Learn to be proud of who you are. This is crucial in developing a strong personality. Every one of us has their own style, their own opinion, but to show it, to live it, to say it, is not so easy. We are too focused on what other people might think about us. We are too focused on whether we could hurt people with what we are doing. Firstly, we shouldn't care too much about what other people think about us and secondly, we can only hurt someone if that person allows us to hurt them. You must learn that you don't have to be ashamed of who you are, or how you look. As long as you're happy with what you see and feel, it's alright. You are the person who has to look into the mirror in the morning and like what it reflects. You shouldn't run with the crowd. Find out what you prefer and like, and who you are, and love yourself for it. When you have found yourself, you have found everything you have ever been looking for, something you will never forget. When you don't want to do something, don't do it, even if others try to convince you. When you want to do something, just do it, it's your life and it's your decision that you have to live with. Be strong and listen to yourself. You will feel great, much better than most people around you because you are living your life, with the emphasis on YOUR life, not that of others. You will always be a leader and never a follower. That is something you can be very proud of. It doesn't matter what you do, you will do it because you want to do it, no pressure, no stress.

Believe me, I don't feel sick anymore concerning anything. I have learned not to justify myself over and over again. I have learned to say what I have to say and not talk behind someone's back. I have learned to wear what I want to wear, do what I want to do. It's just a wonderful feeling because it doesn't matter what happens, I am not afraid to be myself anymore.

Mistakes

A life spent making mistakes is not only more honorable, but more useful than a life spent doing nothing.
Georg Bernard Shaw, Irish dramatist & socialist (1856 - 1950)

If I had to live my life again, I'd make the same mistakes, only sooner.
Tallulah Bankhead, US movie actress (1903 - 1968)

Experience is the name everyone gives to their mistakes.

Oscar Wilde, Lady Windermere's Fan, 1892, Act III
Irish dramatist, novelist, & poet (1854 - 1900)

You must learn from the mistakes of others. You can't possibly live long enough to make them all yourself.

Sam Levenson, (1911 - 1980)

Mistakes make us stronger

The fact that we have problems trusting people, with self-confidence, has something to do with our fear of making mistakes. However, if we never make mistakes, we can't learn, or grow. Nobody likes mistakes because they show us that we have done something wrong. They show us that we are not perfect, but mistakes form our personalities. Mistakes allow us to grow. Children make mistakes over and over again because without them, they wouldn't find their personalities. They learn languages faster than adults because they are not afraid to say a word or sentences wrong a couple of times. They don't see mistakes as something bad, but rather as something normal. It is their basis to learn and to improve. At a certain age, people revert back to the behavior of children. I am sure that this has something to do with self-confidence, since they have had enough life experiences to teach them not to be afraid of what others might think about them. They are not embarrassed of making mistakes. People have expectations and we want to fulfill them. It confuses us in our decisions, and as a consequence, we will make even more wrong decisions. You can take my word for it. We will never be perfect, nobody is. As long as we learn from our mistakes and avoid doing it over and over again, it's okay. Let us make mistakes to learn from them and grow with them!

Failures

Failures don't exist, just mistakes that let you learn and grow.

Failures only exist in your mind, you can't fail!

We have talked about mistakes and most people associate mistakes with failures. I am talking about something that actually doesn't exist for me. Failures are constructs we build up in our minds, but nothing which really exists. We don't fail, we just make mistakes. People see it as the consequence of our mistakes, but it is a negative word and a mistake is nothing negative. If we like, we can say "fail", however, we did nothing more than make a mistake. We lost a fight because we made a mistake, not because we failed. We must get this word out of our minds; it's negative and not necessary in our vocabulary. We will always make mistakes because nobody is perfect!

So, how can a person fail, if he has tried and given his best? That's all a person can do, always give his best. If it doesn't work and he doesn't achieve what he wants, he didn't fail. No, he just didn't achieve what he wanted to, that's all. The experience you take with you is a gain and never a loss, because it helps you to improve. Delete this word; it doesn't exist anymore, not in your life!

I don't want to write any more about it. We only make mistakes, bad mistakes and good mistakes, nothing more ...or less!

Fears

Whatever you fear most has no power - it is your fear that has the power.

Oprah Winfrey, O Magazine
US actress & television talk show host

You gain strength, courage and confidence by every experience in which you really stop to look fear in the face. You are able to say to yourself, 'I have lived through this horror. I can take the next thing that comes along.' You must do the thing you think you cannot do.

Eleanor Roosevelt, US diplomat & reformer (1884 - 1962)

You can't be courageous without fear

"We often develop inferiority complexes and stumble through life with a feeling of insecurity, a lack of self-confidence, and a sense of impending failure. A fear of what life may bring encourages some persons to wander aimlessly along the frittering road of excessive drink and sexual promiscuity. I know this. I know it from my own personal experiences".

Martin Luther King Jr.

Every one of us has fears and they will always be a part of our lives, but it's up to us not to let fear prevent us from living our lives. Martin Luther King Jr. had a dream and this dream was stronger than any fear he had. He overcame his fears because he understood that he could realize his dreams only if he didn't let his fears stop him. People like Martin Luther King Jr. will always be leaders and winners, because they let the positive win. We are humans and we are afraid of the consequences that decisions bring with them, but if we never take a risk to go the way we want to go, despite how strong our fears might be, we will never achieve our goals and never live out our dreams. Fears, which prevent us from living our lives, must be overcome. Challenge yourself by taking action. I was afraid of being alone, so I was alone a lot. I was afraid of flying, so I flew a lot. I overcame most of my fears because I constantly challenged myself by simply doing what I was afraid of. When we were children, we did so many things without having fear, because we didn't know anything about consequences. Our missing life experiences allowed us to be fearless. With everything we did, we discovered what was good for us, and what wasn't. We believed that everything was possible. Sometimes you should approach things as a child would. Don't think about it too much, just do it if you have the feeling that you want to do it. Loose the blockades and use your free mind to achieve your goals, realize your dreams or just live your life. Don't let your fears control your life. You should control your fears!

Loneliness

The worst loneliness is not to be comfortable with yourself.

Mark Twain, US humorist, novelist, short story author, & wit
(1835 - 1910)

At the innermost core of all loneliness is a deep and powerful yearning for union with one's lost self.

Brendan Francis

Be at peace with yourself and you will never be alone again.

If we are not able to control our fear, we are going to be very lonely one day. It will make us lonely, because we are going to avoid situations and people in our lives. Loneliness is the emptiness inside of us. Our hearts feel empty and that makes us feel lonely. This is especially true of successful people because they don't have a lot of real things in their lives. All the success, fame and money can't buy them what they are looking for so badly. It's really like people say: loneliness comes with success. We must learn to find the real things in our lives and take care of them, real things like honest/truthful people. If we look at the news, day after day, we see how people we admire for their success, have to deal with serious drugs and alcohol problems. They can't stand this fake life they live anymore so therefore, they take drugs to forget about it. They go to parties and events because they are addicted to attention. They need it to forget about the emptiness inside of themselves. We are lonely because we are empty. That sounds weird, and it is weird. None of us have to be lonely. We could spend days by ourselves without being lonely. Loneliness has nothing to do with people not being around us all the time, it's the empty feeling in our hearts. We can have thousands of people around us and still feel lonely, or nobody and feel lonely. We have to fill up our hearts with love, and the best love we can have is love for ourselves. We should learn to enjoy all the beautiful things around us that we take for granted. We have to learn to think positively and fill up our hearts to let the emptiness disappear. Enjoy yourself, your life, people who are important to you, the weather and so on. We have to understand that we are not lonely because we are alone. We are lonely because we have lost ourselves. We have closed our eyes and can't see all the beautiful things surrounding us. I can spend days alone by myself. I can go on vacation by myself and feel good. I feel good because I enjoy my life. I enjoy having time for myself. Time in which I can do whatever I want to do without taking care of someone else. If I am at home, I can spend weekends by myself, listening to loud music and dancing through my apartment like a freak, doing well and enjoying everything from the bottom of my heart. I love spending time by myself! I don't have the feeling that I am missing something if I don't go out. I feel good by myself and not at all alone. I know so many people who are in relationships because they can't stand being alone, or who have phony friends because they can't stand being alone.

We must learn to make ourselves the main person we love. We must set ourselves as top priority and then we will never feel lonely again. With everyone else, we should have patience, take our time to learn more about them and decide whether we really want them in our lives or not. When we have reached this point, we don't need someone to be able to feel complete. At this point, it doesn't matter where we are and who is with us, we will not feel empty anymore, an emptiness that is able to kill us. It's a wonderful feeling not to feel lonely, because there is always me, myself and I!

Courage

*Many would be cowards if they had courage
enough.*
Thomas Fuller, English clergyman & historian (1608 - 1661)

*Courage is doing what you're afraid to do. There
can be no courage unless you're scared.*
Eddie Rickenbacker, US WWI aviator & businessman (1890 -
1973)

*It takes courage to grow up and become who you
really are.*
E E Cummings, US poet (1894 - 1962)

*People grow through experience if they meet life
honestly and courageously. This is how character
is built.*
Eleanor Roosevelt, My Day, US diplomat & reformer (1884 -
1962)

Leaders can make a change with courage

Courage is when we overcome something we are afraid of. Every one of us is afraid of different things and to overcome these fears makes us courageous, makes us strong, because we face our problems and face our lives. We won't run away. We will be ready for whatever comes and learn to deal with it. Courage is important because whoever is courageous can live. The ones without it will only exist, but never live. It's exciting, and that is how we should see it, as an adventure. Overcoming our fears makes us proud of ourselves. Well-known people we will never forget changed the world by being courageous. They were leaders for change, people we look up to. If we want to be leaders and not followers, we have to be courageous and go ways other people are afraid to go because of the consequences that could come with it. The world needs people who are courageous, who are not afraid to say what they want to and fight for what they believe in. There are so many people, who have achieved so much with their courage. Those people are the best example that courage always makes a change. Slavery and the discrimination of black people, the Holocaust…all these things would have never happened if people would've been more courageous. These atrocities could have been avoided if courageous people stepped up and built a barrier that could not be broken in front of the tyrants responsible for these heinous acts. People like Hitler knew how to play on people's fear. This is how he, and others like him, were able to achieve any success. We shouldn't allow them to achieve anything! We have to say Stop! We have to say NO! Be courageous without fear. I want to live in a better world. I will do my best to ensure that these things, or other bad things, don't happen again. I will look into a future which is bright. I know I can't change everything by myself, but with this book, I can motivate people to help make a change. Let us be courageous and stand up for the things we believe in. For ourselves, our children and for the rest of the world - for a satisfied life we all can look forward to. Don't let your fears win this battle. We shouldn't be afraid to show people what we feel and what we define as right or wrong for ourselves. Everyone can be courageous. We must forget what others think about us. Let us be courageous to stop the negative and push the positive. Let us make a change.

Sensitivity

The truly creative mind in any field is no more than this: A human creature born abnormally, inhumanely sensitive. To them... a touch is a blow, a sound is a noise, a misfortune is a tragedy, a joy is an ecstasy, a friend is a lover, a lover is a god, and failure is death. Add to this cruelly delicate organism the overpowering necessity to create, create, create -- so that without the creating of music or poetry or books or buildings or something of meaning, their very breath is cut off...They must create, must pour out creation. By some strange, unknown, inward urgency they are not really alive unless they are creating.

Pearl Buck (1892 - 1973)

Sensitivity equals ability

I am sensitive and I am glad that I am. I am proud and thankful for it. A lot of people I know still see it as something negative. They are afraid because they think they could hurt me, but most of them don't actually know what this word means, and the result of nescience is fear and prejudice. Sensitivity means that our senses are more distinctive than those of others. It doesn't mean that we are sitting around 24/7 crying about everything that happens to us. We only feel things more intensively than other people and this can be very helpful and positive, if we know how to use and handle it, and not let it bring us down. A lot of companies have made sensitivity a requirement in getting hired. The business world knows about the advantages of this ability. This ability is crucial, especially in jobs where one has to deal with difficult people and various characters. It's an advantage. Sensitivity allows us to see and feel things faster, which makes it a necessary competence.

When I was a child I cried very often. This is normal for a sensitive child, because they don't know how to use sensitivity in a positive way. We need time and experiences to learn how. I was often angry that I was so sensitive and others weren't. I thought it was a hindrance that wouldn't let me stand through situations. I thought it was something that would prevent me from living my life like I wanted to. Today, I know how to use it and not let it be a disadvantage. I know without it, I would've never made it through the experiences I've been through. It allows me the opportunity to form very good connections to different types of people. Without this sensitivity, it would never have been possible. It's like with every other special talent and ability we have, if we don't know how to handle it and use it correctly, it can be a curse. We feel the good, and the bad things that happen to us very intensely, and we have to learn to handle them. There are still a lot of people who think we can't stand things in comparison to those who are not sensitive. In my opinion, we probably stand through difficult situations even better than they do. We always get a connection to people and situations better than others without sensitivity. Maybe this will help us find solutions for problems much easier. We shouldn't see it as something negative anymore. It's a very important and positive gift we should appreciate. I am proud to have it and I will not apologize for it anymore, because there is nothing to apologize about. I want people to see that we aren't chickens, because we're sensitive. We are just people with strong senses.

Senses

Not the senses I have but what I do with them is my kingdom.
Helen Keller, US blind & deaf educator (1880 - 1968)

Five senses; an incurably abstract intellect; a haphazardly selective memory; a set of preconceptions and assumptions so numerous that I can never examine more than minority of them - never become conscious of them all. How much of total reality can such an apparatus let through?
C.C. Lewis, English essayist & juvenile novelist (1898 - 1963)

I want all my senses engaged. Let me absorb the world's variety and uniqueness.
Maya Angelou, US author & poet (1928 -)

See, hear, smell, feel and taste the beauty

The world is beautiful, and life is beautiful, we just have to see it. Most things are directly in front of us, but we don't notice them. God gave us senses with which we are able to recognize everything. We have eyes to see with. We have ears to hear with. We have a nose to smell with, and a mouth to taste with. He gave us senses so we can experience how beautiful everything is. The problem is that we don't use them the right way anymore. We notice that if we have a cold and our ears are clogged, we don't hear very well. When the cold is gone and our ears are open, we have the feeling that we can hear thousands of times better than before. In fact, we don't hear any better than normal. We are simply more focused on our sense, because we have lost it for a while. It's a good example that shows us that we don't perceive our senses the way we could. We have senses but don't know how to use them. That's sad. If we lived every day like it was our last, believe me, we would use them. We would do it because we want to feel all the beautiful things, want to enjoy them as much as we can. Therefore, we have to learn to use our senses 100 %! Imagine if people were not fat anymore. They would enjoy food and eat healthier, because their sense of taste would tell them that junk food doesn't taste as good as the fresh food we cook ourselves. We would smell how bad the smoke of cigarettes smells and would avoid it. We would hear the peep in our ears when music is too loud and would avoid getting tinnitus. In many ways, we would take much better care of ourselves. Maybe we should think of every day as if it was our last. Maybe then we would wake up and notice everything around us. Live every day like it was your last and every day will be special. We would see things we have never seen before, or better yet, have never recognized before. We would not hesitate, we wouldn't think so much about everything. We would rely more on our senses. We would experience life with everything it has to offer. We would start to be spontaneous and listen to our needs again and trust our senses. We would learn to use our senses again to see, hear, smell, taste and touch how beautiful life is!

Love

It can change everything in a second, used billion of times by billions of people day by day. Emotions let us say it, let us live it, and show it to people we care about. There are so many different situations we need it for. Endless and with hope, we all believe in it. Without it, we couldn't live. We are all looking for it, and trying to keep it once we have finally found it. We take it and give it. Just one word we have already given the biggest meaning…LOVE!

It's always there but not always seen

I always say love is my engine, and I think a lot of people will agree. An engine supplies power, doesn't it? We need power on our way, so let's love one another! Love is like the air we need to breathe, without it we wouldn't survive. Everyone needs it and everyone is looking for it, but why are we looking for love? We don't have to look for it, we just have to open our eyes and we will recognize that it's already with us, all around us. Most people are always searching for love, but they don't recognize that they already have it. Day by day it's there, in their families, circle of friends and other people surrounding them. Love is not one person who is there for you 24/7 and does everything for you. No, it's the most beautiful feeling, a feeling we receive from people who care about us, and the feeling we give to people we care about. So, when we open our eyes and our hearts, we will be surprised to find how much love we are going to get and how much we are able to give. If you love a person, you are able to forget about yourself. You will start to fight for this person, and want to do everything to make this person happy. A lot of people want to have someone who loves them so badly that they start to live in one big illusion. If someone honestly loves you, it doesn't matter how busy this person is, they will find time for you. Women especially always have an excuse for the person they love. He couldn't show me love because of happenings in his childhood, or he is too busy in his job…and so on and so on. It goes as far as women telling me that they were afraid that something might have happened to their husbands or boyfriends, or that they must have lost their phone, when they didn't call. Hellooooo wake uppppp, when someone doesn't show you love, they don't love you. It's better to let them go and stop wasting your time with looking for excuses. It's natural that we have people we feel more connected to than others. When someone doesn't want to learn more about you, doesn't take the time for you, then you should recognize that this person doesn't feel connected, even if you feel so. We should never forget that the people around us are there to give us the love we need. We are not ALONE! A lot of people are not able to love anymore because of their experiences. They are afraid that someone could hurt them. Love is the most beautiful feeling we have and we certainly need it. If we close our hearts, then we also close our hearts to the people who want to love us. When I look at how many people are single, it makes me sick. We are so selfish that we can't forget about ourselves to love anymore. Come on people!!! Open up your hearts and love one another! If you give love, you will get love. I am a perfect example of failing when we talk about love, but I would never give up opening my heart if I have feelings for someone. Honestly, what can I lose? Nobody can hurt me, if I don't let them hurt me. Love doesn't mean that you should give up yourself completely. As long as you stay yourself, love can't hurt you. The mistake people make is to completely change when they like someone. They try to be perfect for this person, but what ends up happening is that the other person loses interest in them. This happens because the other person feels as if the person that they fell in love with is not there anymore! We are playing a role, acting in our own lives, and in that case we are right that someone can hurt us. We give up ourselves but it's not love that hurts us! If I fall in love with someone, I always tell this person "please stay the way you are." Mostly, they laugh and say "yeah, yeah I will remind you of your words that I should stay the way I am". I'm serious about it. I would never fall in love, if I didn't like what I saw in someone. When I think about my last relationship, I realize that the things that drove me crazy are the things I especially miss. Love is important, and if someone wants to show us real love, we should never close ourselves. Otherwise, we are going to miss the most beautiful feeling we have, a feeling that lets us realize everything. Love gives us the power we need. It's the engine of life! We should trust in love, in real love.

Lovesickness

Love is the most beautiful feeling and if we lose someone we love, this love will never be gone. It will live in our hearts and we should be thankful that someone special gave this gift to us. Love is always strength and never weaknesses.

Don't suffer for something that is so beautiful

Whoever knows love also knows about being lovesick. It's always difficult and painful to let someone go who gave us a feeling so incredibly beautiful. A person who made us blind with the feeling they gave us. We are addicted to it and want to have it back so badly, that we get drunk with our desire. However, is it not more the feeling that we want to have back and not the person? When we think about why this person isn't with us anymore, we will see that it was not always perfect between us. Otherwise, they would still be there. We miss this wonderful feeling we had when we were together. So, is it really the person who gave us this feeling? If we look at it closer, we will discover that we gave ourselves this feeling. To be in love makes us blind, we see everything like we want to see it. We are so drunk with the feeling of love that we don't see reality anymore. We don't want anything, or anyone to bother us in this stadium of heaven in which we live. They are the reason, but we are the activator of this feeling. That's why it is said that lovers see the world with rose-colored glasses, glasses the lovers lose the longer they know each other. We should give ourselves this wonderful feeling. When in love, we feel as if we can fly. If we end a relationship, or someone leaves us, we should not replace this good feeling with a bad one. We should be glad and thankful for the wonderful time we had together. Remind ourselves with a smile on our faces whenever we think about these times. This doesn't mean that we shouldn't let our emotions go. No, we have to let them go, but we should never forget the positive things, even if it's tough. Love shouldn't have anything to do with suffering. We are allowed to be sad but we shouldn't suffer. I know the feeling of being lovesick, as most other people do. I overcame it very fast because I focused on the positive things. Even if you think that there could never be something positive about it, the moment you start to look at the situation a little bit closer, you will find something positive. Try to focus on the positive. Every end also brings a new beginning. Enjoy the time with yourself for a while. Do things you always wanted to do, it will help you to sort out your life. You should take this time because very often, we have made plans for the future with our partner, which disappear when the relationship is over. So, make new plans just for yourself and concentrate on them. It will help you to overcome the break-up it a little bit faster.

Jealousy

People that are jealous all the time are too focused on other people's lives and give their own life no chance to become a priority.

A disease you can cure

Another feeling we bring into connection with love is jealousy. A lot of people know this feeling, if they love someone from the bottom of their heart, and they are afraid to lose this person. Jealousy is something we don't need in our lives. We can be jealous, but we can't avoid it if the person we love leaves us, if they want to leave us. Moreover, we give ourselves a hard time. We are sitting somewhere, thinking of all the things this person might do without us, instead of trusting the person we love. We should think about it rationally; if your lover really wants to be with another, they will find a way to be with another. Whether we are jealous or not, it will not change anything about their decision and their needs and wants to fulfill. What is jealousy good for? The answer is...for nothing! People who are jealous keep themselves busy. They are busy the whole time with watching out for everything, checking phone calls, checking credit card bills etc. They are looking for situations in which they can prove that the other person is unfaithful. The probability that the person we love will leave us because of our exhausting behavior is HUGE! None of us are happy if our partner tries to control us all the time. We expect trust. I agree, without trust you can't have a relationship, not a relationship that has a future. None of us want to have a person who doesn't trust us, or a partner who doesn't have trust in themselves. When we are jealous, we don't have trust in ourselves. We think we can't offer this person everything they need. We are probably right because we are just human beings…not God. However, we should at least have enough trust in ourselves that we believe we can offer them important things. This is called confidence. Confidence makes us attractive, and in addition, gives us a good feeling. We shouldn't think about our partner all the time. We should have the opinion that if they're smart, they will know what they have found in us. If not, they should leave. If they don't come to this realization, then they are not the right person who we want to spend the rest of our lives with. If we learn to think this way, we will never have problems with jealousy anymore. We should value ourselves, because we deserve to have value. We shouldn't wait for others to give us value. If they do it, that's great, and if not, they don't deserve to be a part of our lives. Ladies, if we are out with our boyfriends or husbands, and other women start looking at them, or dancing with them, we should be proud that we have men who are so attractive that other people look for their company. We should be proud and not worried, because we are the ones going home with them. We are the people they chose as partners in their lives. We should stop constantly giving ourselves, and them, a bad feeling by being jealous. We should enjoy the time together and see what life brings.

Faith

Where you are tolerated, you are only accepted, but where you are celebrated, you are loved. God celebrates you every day, because he loves you!!!

The real power behind whatever success I have now was something I found within myself - something that's in all of us, I think, a little piece of God just waiting to be discovered.

Tina Turner, O Magazine, December 2003
US singer (1938 -)

You can't see it, but feel it.

If you have faith, you will see the world in another light, bright and beautiful as it is! Faith is nothing you can see or touch. It's something in your heart. I believe in God, and I believe that everything that happens to me in my life has a meaning and God has a reason for it. In situations which hurt me, I ask God why he's doing it to me and of course, there is nobody who speaks to me and gives me the answers. No, God shows me why!

For example: Someone breaks up with you, you feel down and don't understand why. You go out to listen to a performer who sings a song both you and your ex-lover always listened to in the past. While there, you meet a man who becomes your husband one year later. The conclusion is; if we never met the first person, we never would have shared a love of that song, and if we never broke up, we never would have gone to this performance. We would've never met our husband.

Everything in life happens for a reason and even if we don't understand it yet, we will understand it one day.

We just have to keep our eyes open and keep our faith. I love to believe. It gives me power and hope. It also teaches me to be thankful for everything in my life day by day. I can pray wherever I am. I don't need a church, or to even cross my hands. I just need to send my thoughts to God. We have so many different religions, but they all have one thing in common; they all teach us that we are not alone in life. There is someone who goes through the road of life with us. This is a wonderful feeling because no matter what happens in our lives, as long as we keep our faith, we will never be alone. If we look at history, most of the wars that were fought had something to do with people's faiths. I think it's time to stop having religious wars! It doesn't matter which religion we look at, there are none which instructs us to start wars for it. Each and every one of us should have the choice of what they want to believe in or not. We have to feel good about what we are doing, and if we feel good, we want others to do the same so they can feel what we are feeling. We must also accept it if someone doesn't want to believe in the same things we believe in. We should be happy with our faith. It's wonderful that we have it. Faith gives us hope and power and takes away our fears. We should allow people to stay the way they are and be glad that we have found faith for ourselves.

Ambition

Live neither in the past nor in the future, but let each day's work absorb your entire energies, and satisfy your widest ambition.

Sir William Osler, to his students British (Canadian-born) physician (1849 - 1919)

Keep away from people who try to belittle your ambitions. Small people always do that, but the really great make you feel that you, too, can become great.

Mark Twain, US humorist, novelist, short story author, & wit (1835 - 1910)

Ambition - it is the last infirmity of noble minds.

James M. Barrie, Scottish dramatist & novelist (1860 - 1937)

Where there's a will, there's a way

Ambition is the greed of a person for glory, which is often connected with striving for power and glory. In the 16th century, people didn't know the word ambitious, they called it energetic. Ambition is a very strong emotion, which can lead to success, but it is a curse if you can't control it. If you want to get somewhere in your car as fast as you can, you can't always drive at full speed. You have to be considerate of others. With ambition it is the same; you have the power and want to give as much as you can, but there are limits you should be aware of. They are there for a specific reason. Ambition is a strong emotion and that makes it hard to control, but you can avoid the disadvantages if you learn to steer it. I drove a spinning marathon without preparation and finished it. Five weeks later, I ran a marathon without the necessary preparation and finished it. Another three weeks later, I was in a hospital. My ambition let me accomplish my goals, but I risked my health and was close to death. You must always compare what you get (reward) to what you can lose (risk). To lose your life for a goal isn't worth it at all. Your body has limits, and your environment has limits you should be aware of. So, be aware of what you risk and control your ambition to let it work for you in a positive and healthy way.

Patience

Patience has its limits. Take it too far, and its cowardice.

George Jackson, (1941 - 1971)

Good ideas are not adopted automatically. They must be driven into practice with courageous patience.

Hyman Rickover, US (Polish-born) admiral (1900 - 1986)

He that can have patience can have what he will.

Benjamin Franklin, US author, diplomat, inventor, physicist, politician, & printer (1706 - 1790)

Patience is bitter, but its fruit is sweet.

Aristotle, Greek critic, philosopher, physicist, & zoologist (384 BC - 322 BC)

The secret weapon to success

We can't always influence what happens in our lives, or our environment. We can't always take action. Sometimes, we just have to wait and see what happens. A very important person in my life taught me to be patient and showed me the importance of it. I am very thankful for that. It has given me the ability to accept situations that I can't change, and wait on situations which I can't influence. It has made me into a more relaxed person. It's a great feeling not to feel pressure all the time. My mind is free of chaos. This allows me to make better decisions and lets me choose better ways than before. I have learned to wait if it is necessary to wait, and to take action if it is important to take action. I have learned to differentiate, and that makes me stronger, faster and better in everything I do. I feel healthier because I am not under pressure anymore. Patience has become my secret weapon in life, and I hope you will make it yours as well.

Remember, Sometimes it's worth waiting instead of running for nothing and wasting precious energy.

Sometimes, it's good to wait and see what will come instead of driving yourself crazy with predictions. Sometimes, it's just good to have patience...even with yourself!

Balance

The best and safest thing is to keep a balance in your life, acknowledge the great powers around us and in us. If you can do that, and live that way, you are really a wise man.

Euripides, Greek tragic dramatist (484 BC - 406 BC)

As we look deeply within, we understand our perfect balance. There is no fear of the cycle of birth, life and death. For when you stand in the present moment, you are timeless.

Rodney Yee

Our Ying and Yang

You can work as much, and as hard as possible but if you don't know how to keep the balance, you can never bring out the best in you. Body and mind have to be in balance to get 100% productivity; otherwise you will be productive, but just up to a certain point. The interests in Yoga and Meditation have both increased within the last few years. As the economy becomes more and more difficult, and a higher performance is expected from people, the demand for ways that one can fulfill these expectations has risen. Even in our private lives, we have higher demands than years before. Today, you have to be a successful person in business, as well as a parent, spouse or life partner. All these requirements need to be fulfilled and only a balance will make it possible to fulfill these required expectations. Otherwise, you will be burned out quickly with the challenges you have, privately as well as occupationally. There are many different ways to find your balance. I have no secret recipe I can give to you to find it. This is something personal, and the only person who knows what allows you relaxation amidst chaos, is you. Yoga and Meditation are good ways to achieve balance, but not everyone finds the calmness they are looking for from them. Think about what you love to do in your leisure time. Mostly, those are the things which bring forth relaxation. Ying and Yang are more important than ever before. Find your balance and you will find the peace within!

Prejudice

*If we were to wake up some morning and
find that everyone was the same race, creed
and color, we would find some other cause
for prejudice by noon.*

George Aiken

It is never too late to give up our prejudices.

Henry David Thoreau, 'Economy,' Walden, 1854 US
Transcendentalist author (1817 - 1862)

*Opinions founded on prejudice are always
sustained with the greatest of violence.*

Francis Jeffrey, Scottish critic & jurist (1773 - 1850)

You don't know everything, so don't prejudge everything.

Prejudice is the result of missing knowledge. People have it because they don't know the backgrounds of other people or situations, and instead of learning about things and arguing with facts to prove their views and opinions, they prejudge. Our world is not perfect. People are not perfect and prejudice makes everything even worse. We have so many problems in our world, why do we invent new ones? I have travelled a lot and wherever I have been, people thought they knew who I was because they heard something about German culture before. Probably, they heard about typical German habits, but it doesn't mean that I have those. To be able to know more about people, you have to learn more about them as individuals. That's the only way to really know someone. Every person is different independent of skin colour, religion, heritage or financial status. Don't think you know everything about someone, or something right from the beginning. If you think you do, you will miss the opportunity to learn more about people. Ask, listen and learn. Stop prejudging and help to stop others who do so as well. If people recognize that you don't take an interest in their prejudices, they will start to question them. Share your knowledge and let people benefit from what you have learned. You will start to see the world in a new light!

Respect

Some people have so much respect for their superiors they have none left for themselves.

Peter McArthur

Respect yourself and others will respect you.

Confucius, Chinese philosopher & reformer (551 BC - 479 BC)

Every human being, of whatever origin, of whatever station, deserves respect. We must each respect others even as we respect ourselves.

U Thant

You don't have to accept everybody, but you should respect everybody.

The point isn't to accept decisions of others, or to understand different approaches towards life. The point is to respect others and their view of life without consideration of their social background, skin color, or religion.

Every one of us wants to be treated with respect. It is important that we respect each other, or else we wouldn't take each other seriously. But how do we get people to take us seriously? How do we receive respect? The answer is personality! If you know who you are, you have personality. If you know how to handle your emotions, go your way without any excuses, not afraid to take responsibility, and are honest to yourself and others, you have personality. You are real. You are yourself without any doubts! That makes you a very strong person. People see this, feel it, appreciate it, admire you for it, and show you respect. We often hear people ask why nobody treats them with respect. It's all up to you whether you receive respect or not. If you go your way with your own opinion, your own view of life, with your own dreams and goals, people will show you the respect you are looking for. They show you respect because they see that you have personality. They see that you are a person with ambitions and goals in life. By behaving in a certain way, you show others how they should, and can treat you. You are the only person who can build borders that nobody is allowed to break. You are the only person who can show others how you want to be treated. Use this power you are holding in your hands to get what you want…respect. This is something you have to work for. Nobody will give it to you right in the beginning. The more you are willing to work on yourself, the more respect you will receive.

Remember: Give yourself respect and you will receive respect.

Pride

Generosity is giving more than you can, and pride is taking less than you need.

Kahlil Gibran, Lebanese artist & poet in US (1883 - 1931)

When dealing with people, let us remember we are not dealing with creatures of logic. We are dealing with creatures of emotion, creatures bustling with prejudices and motivated by pride and vanity.

Dale Carnegie

Pride breakfasted with plenty, dined with poverty, and supped with infamy.

Benjamin Franklin, US author, diplomat, inventor, physicist, politician, & printer (1706 - 1790)

Pride

Pride is good as long as you keep the balance. If you have pride, you give yourself love for your own excellence. It's always good to value yourself, but don't forget to give it to others as well. Excellence is a strong word and it describes the high opinion you have for yourself. Don't forget that conservativeness is important too, or else you will give others the feeling that you think you are the only one who exist, or matter. Opinions about pride differ. Some believe that it is a positive attitude, while others think it is a negative one. It is a strong feeling, which can evolve into a stimulating pleasure and a feeling of accomplishment. It can have the positive benefits of enhanced creativity, productivity and altruism, which are all important. On the other hand, it can evolve into vanity, arrogance and overestimation of one's own capabilities. These traits can become debilitating. If it is your pride, a national pride, or an ethnic pride, you should be sure to benefit from pride. It is an ability that successful people have and need, but in a controlled way. Don't develop into a dictator. Develop into a positive thinking and successful person who knows how to control their pride, and knows how to use it in a positive way.

Death

But in this world nothing can be said to be certain, except death and taxes.

Benjamin Franklin, Letter to Jean Baptiste Le Roy (1789) US author, diplomat, inventor, physicist, politician, & printer (1706 - 1790)

Death is more universal than life; everyone dies but not everyone lives.
A. Sachs

Do not fear death so much, but rather the inadequate life.

Bertolt Brecht, The Mother, 1932
German Communist & dramatist (1898 - 1956)

I guess that's how death works. It doesn't matter if we're ready or not. It just happens.

Randy K. Milholland, Something Positive, 11-29-2006
Webcomic pioneer

Wherever one road ends another one begins

Most people avoid thinking about death. They avoid talking about death, and I can understand why people don't want to think and talk about it. They are scared to think about it, since they don't know what will happen after they die. Actually, we shouldn't think about what will happen after we are dead. We can't predict what, or who is waiting for us. We just have to wait until our time comes to see what happens. It's always scary for us to deal with something we have no influence over, but death is a part of our life. We all come into this world, and we all have to leave this world. My question is; why do people see everything that they don't understand as something negative? Maybe when we die, we transition to a place that is much better than this world. However it is, we all have to die one day and nobody can predict when, or how it will happen. None of us can avoid dying. I think people have a problem with the idea of leaving everything they have behind. It's always hard to leave people you love, but this is a part of life as well. You find people and you lose people, and in the end it's just you. We don't like the idea that we are totally on our own very well. When we die, it's a journey we have to take by ourselves. If we learn to face ourselves in life, to love ourselves and remind ourselves about the things contained in this book, we will not be so afraid of this journey that we all will have to take individually, when our time comes. You will see it as a part of your life, and as you know…with every end there comes a new beginning. By having a positive attitude, you will be able to make the best of this journey. Live your life as best as you can. Love every second you spend on earth and be thankful for it. I am confident that whatever happens to us when we have to leave this place, it will be nothing bad!

Rejection

In life we don't get what we want, we get in life what we are. If we want more we have to be able to be more, in order to be more you have to face rejection.

Farrah Gray

Accept acceptance, reject rejection

Rejection never feels good and it's nothing we look forward to, but it exists. If you are on your way to success, you will see and feel it more often than you prefer to. The question is; how does one handle the emotions that come with rejection? Maybe you feel hurt in your dignity, in your pride, or you feel like a loser who will never accomplish their goals. Maybe your self- confidence is damaged by it, or you reject the rejection and go on even stronger, and with more ambition than before. Grow with every rejection and show people who rejected you that they were wrong by you succeeding. Whatever you do, whether it's music, write or paint, if people like it or not, it is always in the eye of the beholder. There are always people who reject, and others who accept. Think about the acceptance and forget the rejection. This will give you a better feeling. A lot of famous people like Beethoven and Albert Einstein had been rejected before they became famous. These people never gave up believing in who they were and in what they did. This is what brought them success. If you have the courage to stand up for what you believe in, despite public opinion, then this is what makes YOU a winner. Reject rejection, accept acceptance.

Visualization

*Use your imagination not to scare yourself
to death but to inspire yourself to life.*
Adele Brookman

*I would visualize things coming to me. It
would just make me feel better.
Visualization works if you work hard.
That's the thing. You can't just visualize
and go eat a sandwich.*
Jim Carrey, Oprah Winfrey Show, 1997

Visualize, see and realize

Your brain's RAS (reticular activating system), which filters all the information that streams into your head will let anything in that helps you to achieve your goals. All those goals and dreams you have constantly visualized before. Constant visualization builds pictures into your brain. The more you are able to give these pictures colors and sounds, the more detailed they become and the better the filter functions.

Daydreams, for example, are an important foundation for the achievement of our dreams and goals. They give us the opportunity to build these pictures in our heads. The more often we dream, the clearer the picture will be in the end and the higher the possibility is that our brain will give us the right information we need to materialize these dreams. Paint the picture you see day by day in your head, bring it onto paper, which you can see every day. You will see how helpful this tool will be on your way to realization. Use your brain and use it to 100% of your ability. You will laugh and cry, because you are starting to feel the pictures you see. Don't be scared, the more you feel it, the more you want it. To see your goal is one thing, to feel it is another. It makes everything much more intense, even the passion to realize and achieve it. Use this unbelievable power to help you to realize it. The only thing you have to do is visualize it every day. Visualize it intensively, give your picture colors and sounds, feel it and bring it on paper and place it somewhere you can see it every day. You can visualize at breaks, when you go running, or in the shower. Choose places where you are by yourself and let the emotions you feel during your visualization go. Firstly, it will give you the best feeling ever and secondly, it will give you the power and passion you need to make this vision come true.

Think about your goals! Think about them deeply and not just when you sleep, and you will achieve all of them.

Persistence

Energy and persistence conquer all things.

Benjamin Franklin, US author, diplomat, inventor,
physicist, politician, & printer (1706 - 1790)

Persistence is the twin sister of excellence.
One is a matter of quality; the other, a
matter of time.

Marabel Morgan, The Electric Woman

Never stop walking

It takes as long as it takes. When achieving your goal, you never know when the long and exhausting way you have walked will bring you there. But one thing is sure, the more you walk, the higher the possibility is that you get there. Sometimes you can sprint, at other times, you must slow down, but as long as you follow your road and walk it, you will arrive. There are people who don't have the persistence to walk all the way to the end. They stop somewhere on their road and settle down. Some of them do so in the beginning, others in the middle and a lot of them close to the end. None of us know how close our goals actually are. There are no signs on the road showing us how many miles we still have to go. This not knowing makes persistence so difficult. If you quit, you never will realize your goal. You have a goal which is the most important thing to you, and nobody in this world can tell you when you will accomplish it. As long as you don't give up and you keep walking, every road, as long as it may seem, has an end. Be persistent, be patient and never forget why you are on this road. Then you will achieve what you have been waiting for and working towards for so long. You will meet people on this road who will motivate you to run, others will discourage you and decrease your speed until you creep, but as long as you are persistent, it doesn't matter, because you are never standing still.

Remember: You know your arrival and persistence will let you arrive!

Self-betrayal

All a man can betray is his conscience.

Joseph Conrad, English (Polish-Ukrainian-born) novelist
(1857 - 1924)

*When you betray somebody else, you also
betray yourself.*

Isaac Bashevis Singer, New York Times Magazine, Mar.
12, 1978, US (Polish-born) Jewish author (1904 - 1991)

*Love God and trust your feelings. Be loyal
to them. Don't betray them.*

Robert C. Pollock

See a person as a person and not like a person in his function

We have started to see people as unappreciative, inconsiderate, and insensitive...but are they? Is it just the picture we have of them, to give us a more positive one of ourselves? Are we merely trying to justify our own wrong behaviour by not seeing and treating them as "human beings" with needs and feelings as we have and deserve? Wouldn't we feel better if we didn't blame and judge others just to have a reason for wrong decisions we have made? If we betray ourselves, we begin to see the world in a way which justifies our self-betrayal. We see ourselves and others in a systematically distorted way. They become more objects of our thoughts rather than humans. How will we ever be successful in our jobs, relationships and friendships, if we are not able to see people as human beings? To work as a leader, you have to understand your team. Without your team, you can't be a leader. Wouldn't you get better production from your team if you showed them that, independent of everybody's position, you have one aspect in common, namely being human beings with goals and needs?

If you don't see your partner as a person, but as a partner in his function, you will have a relation but never a relationship. If it doesn't work in your job or relationship, you will find a reason for why the others failed. You lie to yourself to feel better with failing in "your" humanity! We make our lives more stressful and complicated because we think we know what we don't know and see what we don't see. This distorted picture in our heads will become clear the moment we learn to see each person for who they are and treat them accordingly. Our point of view will change!

You know me because you know me and see me because you see me, deeply and truly.

Criticism

If you are not criticized, you
may not be doing much.
Donald H. Rumsfeld (1932 -), Secretary of Defense

Against criticism a man can
neither protest nor defend
himself; he must act in spite of
it, and then it will gradually
yield to him.
Johann Wolfgang von Goethe (1749 - 1832)

People ask for criticism, but
they only want praise.
W. Somerset Maugham (1874 - 1965)

Improve with ever criticism

I have never liked criticism, but I have learned the importance of it. I will never forget the first time in my business life, when I got criticism and how I felt. I was so angry, hurt and disappointed. I couldn't understand why people saw it as an important tool on the way to success. I thought that something that brought so much negative energy up couldn't be good, in my opinion...but my opinion would change. One day an executive asked me this question: "Do you think I would waste my time with critique, if I didn't see your potential to make something average to something good, and something good to something great?" At that moment, I understood that nobody in business would ever waste time to criticize me, if they didn't see any potential in me. My view changed. Today, I know it gives me the chance to improve, to see another perspective, and to see how others see me. That helps me grow! You will not always have influence on the person who criticizes you and the way that they do it. Therefore, it can be tough! Most people don't choose the sensitive way to criticize you. However, you always have influence on your attitude towards it. You know that you would never be sitting there if they didn't see any potential in you. You are worth it and you should remember that in every moment, in which it gets tough, it will help you to handle difficult and non constructive criticism better. Don't see it as an attack and defend yourself, see it as a chance to improve, grow and listen very well. Nobody can hurt you, if you don't allow them to hurt you. So don't be afraid, be focused and listen. Criticism can be tough, but with the right attitude you will learn to pick out the positive and ignore the negative aspects.

To give criticism is as difficult as receiving it. The only difference is that we are not as afraid of giving criticism as of receiving it. Every one of us, who was in a situation to give criticism, knows how difficult it can be. Start with something positive, explain to the person you criticize at the start what you like before you switch over to what the person could make better. Thereby you avoid a defensive demeanour from the person who receives the criticism. If the person listens to you and thinks about what you have said, you have achieved your objective and you were successful. Remember: Don't see criticism as something negative anymore. See it as a chance to make something good to something great and something great, to something special!!!

Attachment

May I introduce myself?

You say I am not perfect.

Yes, you are right and I am proud of it, because I am real!

Everything you see, everything you read is 100% me.

Games you play on the field, not in life!

You don't like what you see?

Fine, you don't have to take it

It's up to you to leave.

I made mistakes in my life

and I will make new ones,

because I learn from them,

they let me grow

and let me find my way.

I don't regret anything I did,

because I can't change it.

But I can avoid doing it again.

I can face others,

because I can face myself.

I am honest to others,

because I am honest to myself.

I am not an actor in my own life.

My eyes are open,

I see problems and I try to find solutions.

I have fears,

positive fears God gave me to protect myself,

and negative ones I overcome day by day.

I am not afraid to go my way,

life is a challenge I will deal with.

Thanks to the haters for hating me for what I have achieved.

Pity you get for free, for envy you must work!

Thanks to the people who love me.

You are my engine in life and I appreciate your love so much.

And do you know what? It's a wonderful feeling just to be myself and not to be perfect!

Create yourself

Your thoughts created you to be the person you are today, and you create your thoughts. Always think positively and remember; you are what you think. If you create yourself, you should never forget that every stone is important. Without the lower stones you will never be able to build the wall to its highest point. Create your individuality because if everyone becomes the same sort of stone, which can only be used in the middle of the wall, you would just have spires which can drop. Build walls that nobody can break. Your work on yourself is a stone, which can build something, but to find yourself in the end is a wall with a strong foundation.

Gratefulness

If you just focused on the big things in life, you forget to appreciate the small ones. You can't find God in the big moments of your life, you find him in every little moment of it. If you're thankful for yesterday, appreciate today and you will see the beauty of tomorrow. If you live every second, you will find the minute and appreciate the hour. Life is not about creating something big, it's about creating yourself and being thankful for what it brings you.

Our beauty lies within our differences

Every character has a story to tell, a heart to show and something to hide, regardless of skin colour, religion, and opinion or style. If you look closer and listen more attentively, you are going to see that our beauty lies within our differences. One man's weakness is another man's strength. We complement one another and if you take some time to talk with people, you wouldn't normally talk with, and look at people you wouldn't normally look at, you would see a world which is so incredibly beautiful, exciting and interesting, a world like you haven't seen it before. Stop judging, stop hating and stop seeing the negative aspects of life. Whenever you look behind the scenes, you will see the positive parts and you will understand what I mean when I say our beauty lies within our differences. We are different, which makes us strong and together we are ONE!

Reminder of a Hero

I have a dream. With this speech, Martin Luther King, Jr. made the hopes of two hundred and fifty thousand people, gathered at the Lincoln Memorial in Washington, D.C., come true. It was the largest civil rights demonstration ever held in the USA. These words spoken by a man who believed in the positive and who fought for what he believed in. People around the world stopped breathing when he spoke. The words he used were honest ones. He believed in the beauty of truth. He taught us what it means to be discriminated against, and that we all must learn to live together, or else we will all perish as fools[1]. He showed us that forgiveness is not an occasional act, but rather a permanent attitude. Martin Luther King Jr. was the one, who told us that it may well be that the greatest tragedy of this period of social transition movement is not the glaring noisiness of the so-called bad people, but the appalling silence of the so-called good people. By being silent, we agree and whatever affects one directly, affects everyone indirectly. Our strength lays in our differences. Whatever is one's weakness is another's strength. He believed that there is an amazing potential for goodness within human nature and he never gave up his belief that the important thing about a person is not the sex, religion, skin colour or hair texture, but the texture and quality of one's soul. If we look at his life, we can see that it is definitely hard to fight for the positive, but even harder to live with the negative. He was a man who knew that the ultimate measure of a person is not where he stands in moments of comfort and convenience, but where he stands at times of challenge and controversy. Hate begets hate, violence begets violence[1]. We must meet the force of hate with the power of love, and we must use time creatively and realize that the time is always ripe to do right. This man has given his life to fight for the rights of human beings, so that others could start to have a life. It was he, who said that we must rapidly begin the shift from a "materially-oriented society" to a "human-oriented society". He also argues that if machines and computers, profit motives and property rights are considered more important than people, the giant triples of racism, materialism and militarism are incapable of being conquered. Martin Luther King, Jr. will always be alive in our hearts. His words of wisdom will help us to stand up for the positive and fight for the people who can't fight for themselves. The self cannot be self without other selves[1]. A tribute to a man, who will never be forgotten: Martin Luther King, Jr.

1 Martin Luther King Jr.

Always seen but never recognized

This chapter is dedicated to all the homeless people out there, fighting day by day to survive. The people we always see, but never recognize. God bless you all out there on the streets!

Your home the street,
day by day looking for a place to sleep.
This pain so deep, day and night
even when you see the sun it's not bright.
Tears rolling over your face,
there where you sit with your space.
Over and over prayers you sing,
the belief in better days, in a new begin.
No protection at night, just fears,
enemies nearly everyone, bring out more tears.
Endless pain, hunger you have to fight with,

no other chance, for you it is what it is.

You know every face from your street

but nobody knows yours, nobody you meet.

Hoping for a human reaction

a little smile, a good morning or goodbye.

You're always seen but never recognized.

People all over, people with a heart of ice.

You have no material things to offer

human behaviour let you even more suffer.

Wishes for a smile, a good morning or goodbye.

You look up to the sky, asking God why.

You use to work before,

don't have anything anymore.

You lost your job and house,

all you had including your spouse.

You know how a normal life is,

know what you had, and know what you miss.

Now you are not there anymore,

they don't know where they should use you for.

Nobody wants to hold your hand,

dirty, not good enough for the upper class stand.

Lost on your road, people you adore

they have a life, one worth to be alive for.

Alcohol let forget reality,

let you feel far away, let you feel free.

Hoping for a human reaction

a little smile, a good morning or goodbye.

You're always seen but never recognized.

People all over people with a heart of ice.

You have no material things to offer

human behaviour let you even more suffer.

Wishes for a smile, a good morning or goodbye.

You look up to the sky, asking God why.

It was snowing again this night on your street

when you closed your eyes to sleep.

Pain from the cold of the weather,

of the people, whatever.

You closed your eyes, didn't open them anymore,

that's what nobody deserved,

that's what nobody should living for.

Lonely you went to your last sleep,

lonely you died there on your street.

They found you the next day,

pick you up to throw you away.

He was hoping for a human reaction

a little smile, a good morning or goodbye.

You were always seen but never recognized.

People all over, people with a heart of ice.

You had no material things to offer,

human behaviour let you even more suffer.

Wishes for a smile, a good morning or goodbye.

You were looking up to the sky, asking God why.

Nobody was there

was there when you died

nobody to hold your hand

nobody to say goodbye.

I won't because I will!

I won't step into other people's shoes because I want to run faster than them...I won't take the road others take, because I want to leave my footprints on a new one...I won't be the thunder, because the lightning is the one who has the power...I won't think I am someone, because I will be someone ...I won't avoid the fall, because I will learn to stand up again...I won't give a speech, because I will put on a show...I won't give up doing what I do, because I want it to exists...I won't, because I will!!!

With every night comes a new day!

With every night comes a new day
With every end comes a new beginning
The past is gone,
the future unknown
but the present lies in my hand
and I will live this moment,
will live this day as best as I can.
I will not regret what has happened
I can't change it anymore
but I will learn from my mistakes
Just for today and now.
I will not predict what comes next
but I will live free of expectations
I will accept what I can't influence
and will change what I can influence.

I will treat people with the same respect I want to be
treated with,
I will love myself for the person I am
and will love others for that what they are.
Just for today and now.
Yes, the present is now,
and right now I have the chance to give my best,
Just for today and now.
The present which comes out of my past
and leads me into my future.
My present, my moment, for now.
And tomorrow will be another present
and today just another part of my past.
With every night comes a new day.
And with every end a new beginning.

Music

Music is emotion. It's a language everybody understands, because it's something you can feel. It doesn't matter whether you are rich, poor, and famous or not, we all have to handle the same emotions. We all know love, anger and pain. It goes with us through every emotion. We laugh with it and we cry with it. It helps us to stand up if we are down. It helps us to feel understood when we feel alone. We let go of feelings with music. We let them start with music. We sing in church, in the shower, in the club, or on the streets to express ourselves through music. We share memories with it. Music lets us remind ourselves, it shapes us, lets us live. Music is power, it brings people together. It's the language of us all. It's a worldwide connection nobody can break. As long as humans exist, music will exist, because it reflects our emotions, and without emotions we can't live!

Believe in the power of music and let it help you to live your emotions, and be there with your life.

Life

In the moment we begin to live our life we begin to understand what it is about.

Every experience we make will bring us another answer to our questions.

And in the moment we begin to understand what life is about, we begin to live it to the fullest.